D0793294

DIGGING INTO HISTORY

SOLVING THE MYSTERIES OF
MACHU PICCHU

Anita Croy

 **Marshall Cavendish**
Benchmark
New York

Marshall Cavendish Benchmark
99 White Plains Road
Tarrytown, New York 10591
www.marshallcavendish.us

© The Brown Reference Group plc 2009

This edition published in 2009 by Marshall Cavendish Corporation

All rights reserved. No part of this book may be reproduced or utilized in any
form or by any means electronic or mechanical, including photocopying, recording,
or by any information storage and retrieval system, without permission from the copyright holders.

All Web sites were available and accurate when sent to press.

Library of Congress Cataloging-in-Publication Data

Croy, Anita.
Solving the mysteries of Machu Picchu / by Anita Croy.
p. cm. -- (Digging into history)
Includes bibliographical references and index.
ISBN 978-0-7614-3103-9
1. Machu Picchu Site (Peru)--Juvenile literature. 2. Incas--Juvenile literature.
3. Inca architecture--Juvenile literature. I. Title.
F3429.1.M3C76 2009
985'.37--dc22
2008004074

Picture credits
Front Cover: Shutterstock: Jarno Gonzalez Zarraonandia

The photographs in this book are used by permission and through the courtesy of:
Art Archive: Mireille Vautier 22; **Bridgeman Art Library:** New York Historical Society 13; **Corbis:** Thorne Anderson 15,
Ali Jarekji 14, Craig Lovell 19, Kazuyoshi Nomachi 24, Pilar Olivares 26-27, Galen Rowell 29, John Van Hassett 9, 28,
Brian A. Vikander 10; **NGIC:** 5, Maria Stenzel 12; **Shutterstock:** 4, Bryan Busovicki 1, 6, 11, Steve Reineck 8,
Joel Shawn 20, 21, Jarno Gonzalez Zarraonanda 6, 16, 18; **Werner Forman Archive:** 25.

Marshall Cavendish Editor: Megan Comerford
Marshall Cavendish Publisher: Michelle Bisson

Series created by The Brown Reference Group plc
www.brownreference.com
Designer: Dave Allen
Picture Researcher: Clare Newman
Managing Editor: Tim Cooke
Indexer: Kay Ollerenshaw

Printed in China
1 3 5 6 4 2

Contents

WHO FOUND THE LOST CITY?

AT THE START OF THE 20TH CENTURY, ONLY LOCALS KNEW ABOUT MACHU PICCHU. THAT CHANGED AFTER THE REMOTE SITE WAS "DISCOVERED" BY ARCHAEOLOGISTS.

At about midday on July 24, 1911, Yale professor Hiram Bingham reached a small hut about 2,000 feet above the roaring Urubamba River in the central Andes of Peru. A very difficult climb had led Bingham and his assistants to a small settlement of Andean Indians high up on a ridge between mountain peaks. Two local men led Bingham to a place covered with stone ruins. He realized at once that this was a spectacular discovery—but he was mistaken in what the discovery was. From the skilled stonework of the ruins, Bingham decided that he had found the lost city of the Inca, Vilcabamba.

Bingham had indeed found an ancient Incan city. It had escaped discovery by the **conquistadors** who conquered Peru in the fifteenth century. The site had not been **looted**. But this was not Vilcabamba—it was Machu Picchu. Today it is one of the most famous ancient sites in the world.

Bingham was not the first person to find the ruined city. In fact, Peruvian farmers lived among the ruins, and three climbers had scratched their names on a rock when they reached the site on July 14, 1901. However, Bingham was responsible for bringing the ruins to the world's attention.

HIDDEN IN THE MOUNTAINS

Few people had seen Machu Picchu since it was abruptly abandoned by the Inca in the sixteenth century. The reason the

Hiram Bingham (1875–1956)

The son of a missionary family, Hiram Bingham (at right in photo) was born in Honolulu, Hawaii. He was well educated and taught Latin American history at Yale University. He was first attracted to South America because of his research into the liberator, Simón Bolívar. Following his marriage to an heiress, Bingham found his direction changed. With his new wealth he was able to pursue his passion for Latin American **archaeology**. He funded five expeditions to explore ancient sites.

Later in his life Bingham became a U.S. senator from Connecticut.

ABOVE: *The Urubamba winds through a valley far below the site of Machu Picchu. The Inca believed the river valley was a sacred place.*

granite rocks with sheer cliffs that fall into fast-moving rapids of the Urubamba River, so there was no easy way to get to the ruins.

The Inca most probably chose the site for the city because it is protected on three sides by a loop in the river far below. On the fourth side is the cliff face of the mountain Huayna Picchu.

A MYSTERIOUS CITY

Nearly a century after Bingham's arrival, Machu Picchu is still full of mysteries. How did Incan builders carry the massive limestone rocks up the mountain? Why did people build a city in such a remote spot? One suggestion was that it was an Incan ruler's retreat during the cold Andean winters. It was at a lower **elevation**, and therefore warmer, than the Incan capital at Cusco.

The most convincing **theory** is that Machu Picchu was a religious and ceremonial center. It is too remote to be a center for trade or a government complex. Archaeologists think the impressive stone architecture is a sign that it was **sacred**.

Machu Picchu was the most magnificent of a string of structures deep

ruins had not been more widely known about sooner was simple: they were very hard to reach. The Inca built their city on top of a steep mountain. The huge canyon of the Urubamba Valley has

in the Urubamba Valley. Archaeologists guess that the remote city was part of a hidden region that was unknown not just to the Spanish, but also to the rest of the Incan Empire.

HISTORY OF DISCOVERY

The Inca abandoned Machu Picchu around the early or mid-sixteenth century. Vegetation soon reclaimed the site. Orchids, lush ferns, and vines grew over the stone buildings. The straw roofs rotted and disappeared.

On his visit in July 1911, Bingham could not fully explore the site. Apart from the terraces where local farmers were growing crops, it was covered in undergrowth. Bingham returned to the United States, where he put together an expedition to excavate the site. The National Geographic Society sponsored nearly four years of work to clear and record the site. The society also used a whole issue of *National Geographic* magazine to describe Bingham's discovery. Machu Picchu was back on the map after nearly 400 years.

BELOW: *The Incan architects designed impressive buildings and temples. Builders were so skilled that no mortar was needed to hold stones together.*

Living With Heritage

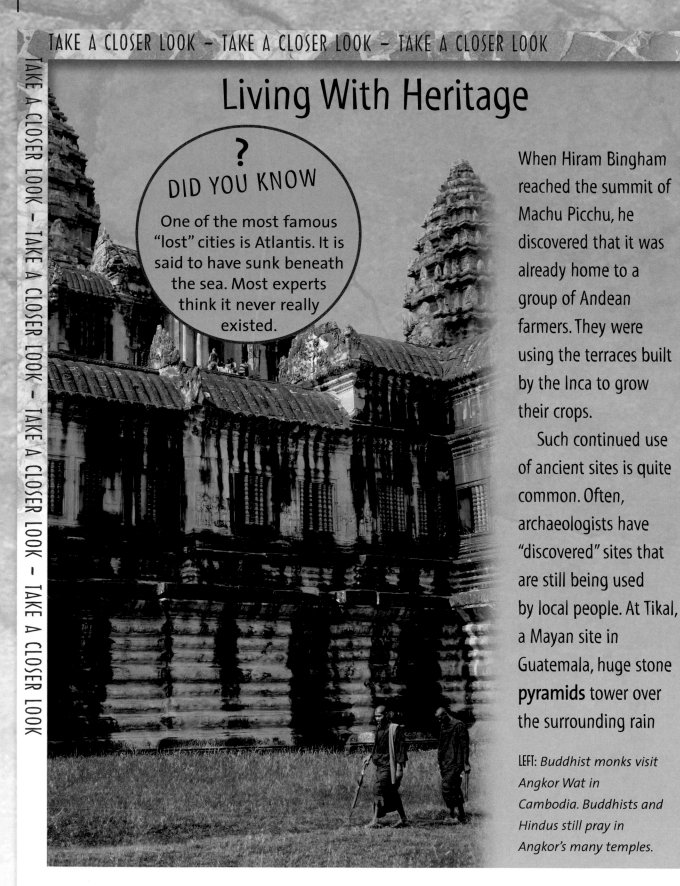

?

DID YOU KNOW

One of the most famous "lost" cities is Atlantis. It is said to have sunk beneath the sea. Most experts think it never really existed.

When Hiram Bingham reached the summit of Machu Picchu, he discovered that it was already home to a group of Andean farmers. They were using the terraces built by the Inca to grow their crops.

Such continued use of ancient sites is quite common. Often, archaeologists have "discovered" sites that are still being used by local people. At Tikal, a Mayan site in Guatemala, huge stone **pyramids** tower over the surrounding rain

LEFT: *Buddhist monks visit Angkor Wat in Cambodia. Buddhists and Hindus still pray in Angkor's many temples.*

EL INSTITUTO NACIONAL DE CULTURA
CUSCO
RINDE HOMENAJE A MELCHOR
ARTEAGA   RICHARTE   Y
ALVAREZ QUIENES HABITARON
EN MACHUPICCHU ANTES DE
HIRAM BINGHAM

OCTUBRE 1993

ABOVE: *A monument erected at Machu Picchu in 1993 commemorates the local men who lived at the site before its "discovery" by Hiram Bingham.*

forest. When outsiders first reached the site, local people were using the temple structures for shelter. In 1946 at Bonampak, a Mayan site in Honduras, local people showed a U.S. filmmaker colorful **murals** that had been preserved on the walls inside a temple. They still used the temple for religious ceremonies, even though its precise purpose had long been forgotten.

Local people often respect sites like Machu Picchu, Tikal, and Bonampak. Even if they do not know what **monuments** were for, or even who built them, they still recognize them as part of their cultural **heritage** and part of their everyday life. At Angkor Wat in Cambodia, for example, Buddhist and Hindu priests pray in the temples built by their Khmer ancestors many centuries ago.

WHO BUILT THE LOST CITY?

MACHU PICCHU WAS ONLY ONE ACHIEVEMENT OF A GREAT EMPIRE THAT DOMINATED MUCH OF PERU FOR A CENTURY—THE INCA.

When the Spanish conquistadors arrived in the Incan capital of Cusco, they were amazed. They found a city of remarkable buildings and temples decorated with gold. The Incan buildings stood on huge blocks of stone that fit together so well it was impossible to slide a knife blade between them. Incan walls can still be seen in Cusco today.

In little less that one hundred years, from 1438 to 1532, the Inca grew from a small tribe to become the dominant people in South America. When the conquistadors arrived in 1532, the Incan

RIGHT: *An Incan road still leads up the side of a steep mountain in the Andes. The empire was held together by a network of roads that crossed mountains, deserts, and thick forests.*

Master Builders

The Inca had no iron tools for building. They shaped limestone boulders using only stone hammers and bronze crowbars. The conquistadors knocked down as many Incan buildings in Cusco as they could. But the buildings' **foundations** were so strongly built that the Spanish simply built their churches and palaces on top of them. The Incan foundations still stand today and have withstood many earthquakes.

BELOW: *The Inca carefully shaped stone blocks to fit together tightly without any kind of cement.*

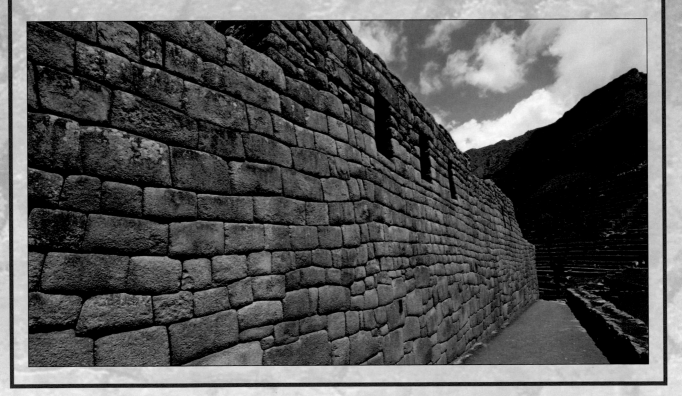

Empire stretched from Colombia in the north to Chile in the south. How Incan power grew so quickly is still a mystery.

Archaeologists know that the Inca were a small tribe who settled at Cusco during the thirteenth century. They date the rise of the Inca to the reign of Pachacuti, who ruled from 1438 to 1471. He oversaw a rapid expansion and ordered the building of roads across the empire. At its peak, the Incan road system covered between 10,000 and

The Ice Maiden

High on the icy slopes of Peru's Nevado Ampato volcano, an amazing discovery lay undisturbed for more than 500 years. In 1995 high-altitude archaeologist Dr. Johan Reinhard found a frozen Incan child near the top of the mountain. He named the **mummy** Juanita.

Tests showed that Juanita was 500 years old. Dressed in her best clothes, she had been left on the mountain as a **sacrifice** to the gods. Scientists learned a lot from Juanita's frozen body. They found that she ate a meal of vegetables before she died. A blow to the side of her head killed her. Her hair was dated to reveal she lived around 1470. Tests on her teeth showed that she was about fourteen years old when she died.

BELOW: *Scientists prepare Juanita for a CAT scan. The medical scanner used X-rays to build a 3-D picture of the mummy and reveal information about how the young girl died.*

14,000 miles (16,000 to 22,500 kilometers). The roads crossed mountains, jungle, and desert. Messengers used the roads to carry messages to and from Cusco. Travelers could sleep in rest houses that lined the route.

RUNNING THE EMPIRE

As the Inca expanded their empire, they forced the people they conquered to pay a **tax** known as *mit'a*. The tax took the form of food or labor. This allowed the Inca to feed a population that may have numbered as many as ten million people.

The Spanish were astonished to learn that the Inca ran their huge empire without any form of writing. The Inca kept records with a system of colored knotted strings known as *quipu*.

HOME OF THE INCA

Cusco means "navel" in the Quechua language of the Inca. The city lay surrounded by mountains, like a belly button. According to an Incan myth, the first people were created there.

Cusco was the home of the Incan king and royal family. Only the royal family and government officials lived in the city, which was designed in the shape of a **puma**. The workers lived outside the city walls. In the center of Cusco stood the Temple of the Sun. The magnificent building had life-sized solid-gold animals and corn plants in its gardens. The conquistadors seized the gold and melted it down to send back to Spain.

The temple was so spectacular because it was central to Incan beliefs. The Inca worshipped the Sun and made sacrifices to the Sun and other gods. Human sacrifice—even of young children—was an important part of the Incan religion. It was considered a great honor to be offered to the gods.

BELOW: *A Spanish painting of Pachacuti, the leader who began the rapid expansion of the Inca in 1438.*

Looting!

One of the biggest problems facing archaeologists is the loss of **artifacts** from ancient sites. Local people often use ancient sites as places to relax. Families have picnics there or children play amid the ruins. At Machu Picchu, families were still farming on the Incan terraces when Hiram Bingham arrived. He also found evidence of fires in many of the buildings, which had been used for shelter.

?
DID YOU KNOW

Museums do not want to return objects they have had for centuries. They say that they bought them fairly, so they were not "looted."

BELOW: *These tablets of early writing were stolen in Iraq—but recovered.*

14

Over time, a site gets worn away. Objects get moved, broken, or even removed.

STEALING TO ORDER

Accidental damage is less of a problem than deliberate looting—the removal of artifacts, often to be sold. Some Peruvians argue that Bingham himself was the first to loot Machu Picchu. He removed about 5,000 artifacts and took them to Yale University. In 2007, Yale finally agreed to return the artifacts to Peru.

Today, objects are stolen from sites to sell to collectors or museums around the world. In Peru, about 100,000 tombs—half of all known Incan sites—have been looted.

GLOBAL PROBLEM

The problem is not just limited to Peru. Almost every ancient site around the world has been affected: It is too expensive to guard the

ruins. For example, people have stolen many of the best sculptures from Angkor Wat and nearby temples in Cambodia, a country plagued by warfare and poverty. Theft continues today. Sometimes looters find temples or other sites and remove artifacts before experts even know the site exists.

STOPPING THE ROBBERS

Archaeologists are trying hard to stop looting. Police forces from different countries now cooperate to stop the illegal trade of artifacts. In June 1999, for example, police retrieved ninety-three Buddha heads that had been taken from Angkor. Many museums and galleries are returning items that were originally stolen. On October 30, 2007, for example, Princeton University signed an agreement to return several looted antiques to Italy.

BELOW: *This carving by the Kushan of Central Asia was looted during fighting in Afghanistan in the 1980s.*

WHY WAS MACHU PICCHU BUILT?

MACHU PICCHU WAS NO ORDINARY CITY. FEW PEOPLE EVER LIVED THERE.
SO WHY DID THE INCA BUILD IT SO CAREFULLY?

When Hiram Bingham reached the jungle-covered ruins of Machu Picchu, he thought that he had discovered Vilcabamba. He based all of his later investigations and ideas on the belief that he had found the lost city. Bingham turned out to be wrong—but his mistake was an easy one to make.

Vilcabamba was famous as the last refuge of the rebel Incas who fled to the Andes to escape the conquistadors. The location of Vilcabamba was not known, but explorers and adventurers had been attracted to

Sacred Alignments

Clues to the purpose of Machu Picchu might be found in some of the world's other ancient sites. Around the globe, early peoples built monuments to **align** with heavenly bodies: the Sun, moon, stars, or planets. From India to Egypt, buildings reflected the importance of **astronomy**, probably because it had a religious element.

Like many other cultures, the Inca worshipped the Sun. The Sun was important in ancient cultures because farmers needed to know when to plant and harvest their crops. They found out by carefully observing the passage of the Sun through the sky. The Pueblo people of southwestern North America, for example, aligned buildings to help chart the Sun's position during the changing seasons.

The Inca believed their ruler, called the Sapa Inca, was the son of the Sun and its earthly representative. The layout of Machu Picchu reflects the importance of the Sun. The central monument at the site was the Hitching Post of the Sun, where a priest would perform a **ritual** to catch the Sun on the winter solstice so it would return for another year. The Temple of the Sun was aligned so that the Sun shone through its windows on the summer solstice, the longest day of the year.

Peru for years to search for the mythical Lost City of the Inca. The site of Vilcabamba was finally located in 1964. Another American explorer, Gene Savoy,

LEFT: *The Hitching Post of the Sun was one of the most sacred Incan sites. As the Sun grew lower in the sky in winter, priests performed ceremonies to make sure that it did not disappear forever.*

discovered the city ruins at Espíritu Pampa, about 60 miles (100 km) west of Machu Picchu.

Bingham explored Machu Picchu from 1911 to 1915. He discovered a number of other nearby Incan sites and an Incan road. The road now forms the Inca Trail, a popular hike for tourists visiting Machu

Picchu. But Bingham did not guess that Machu Picchu was not just a lost city, but a lost region.

A WELL-KEPT SECRET

It is a mystery why the Spanish never found Machu Picchu. If they had known of its existence, they would have destroyed it, as they did other Incan sites. They wanted to wipe out Incan culture as they took over the empire.

There are many theories about Machu Picchu's survival. One is that, at the time of the conquest, not even local people knew of its existence. How was that possible? The Inca may have deliberately kept no records of Machu Picchu. The site was so special that they wanted to hide it. Machu Picchu was built, occupied, and abandoned in only a hundred years. Then, perhaps, it was forgotten—even by the Inca.

BELOW: *Terraces on the steep slopes at Machu Picchu allowed farmers to grow crops—far more crops than the population could consume.*

ABOVE: *The circular tower of the Temple of the Sun has some of Machu Picchu's best stonework. It was probably used for astronomical observations. Its base forms a cavern called the Royal Tomb, though no bodies are there.*

The quality of the city's stonework has led archaeologists to conclude that the city had a ceremonial or spiritual purpose. There were only 200 buildings, so its population was not very large. Yet there are many terraces. These flat steps were dug into the hillsides to enable farmers to grow crops. The terraces at Machu Picchu could have grown far more food than the number of people who lived there would have needed.

FEMALE BONES

When Bingham excavated Machu Picchu, he found remains of about one hundred human skeletons. He thought that 75 percent of the remains were female. From this, he concluded that Machu Picchu was a sanctuary, or religious area, for priestesses known as the Virgins of the Sun of Cusco. Later archaeologists have dismissed this idea. They point out that the only bones Bingham found were

The Sacred Valley

The isolated valley of the Urubamba River is notable for its lush tropical vegetation, steep hillsides, and deep valleys. The number of ceremonial Incan sites built along the valley strongly indicates that it had a spiritual significance to the Inca. Today it is known as the Sacred Valley. Its importance may have reflected its vital role in food production. Both the valley and the high cliff-side terraces were used for growing corn.

Some of the sites dotted along the valley have similarities to Machu Picchu. At Pisac, for example, there is a temple that has its own "hitching post." Other ruins in the Sacred Valley include temples to the Sun, moon, rainbows, rain, and stars.

The surviving foundations at Ollantaytambo reveal the careful planning of the Incan city. It was divided into blocks, each of which was built around a central courtyard. Accounts left by the Spanish record that the defeated Inca took refuge there before they were driven farther into the mountains.

RIGHT: *Just 10 miles (16 km) outside Cusco, the Sacred Valley is home to the most important Incan monuments, including Machu Picchu.*

skulls. Determining the sex of a person from a skull alone is very difficult.

SACRED CLUES

Clues at Machu Picchu suggest that it had a religious purpose. One is the Hitching Post of the Sun, or *Intihuatana*. This rock has a jutting projection that seems to have been used in rituals connected with the Sun.

The site seems to have been chosen to give the widest possible view of the sky overhead—and therefore the Sun—and the surrounding mountains. Visitors entering the main gate look across the Sacred Plaza to a stunning view of the mountains. The Temple of the Three Windows faces the Sun on the summer solstice, the year's longest day. On the far side of the plaza, the Cave of the Sun, or *Intimachay*, faces the Sun on the winter solstice, the shortest day.

In addition to worshipping the Sun, the Inca may also have worshipped the mountains. They understood that mountains were closely linked to the changeable weather of the region. The mountains were therefore essential to ensuring the rainfall that the Inca needed to keep their terraced fields fertile.

Modern archaeologists are fairly certain that Machu Picchu was a ceremonial center for a large region. The number of ruins found across the Sacred Valley supports this theory.

BELOW: *The Inca grew many varieties of corn. In a region with little farmland, corn was an important part of the Incan diet.*

WHAT HAPPENED TO MACHU PICCHU?

THE INCA ABANDONED MACHU PICCHU LESS THAN A CENTURY AFTER THEY BUILT IT. BY THEN, SPANISH INVADERS HAD OVERRUN MUCH OF THE EMPIRE.

The Spanish came to Peru looking for treasure. When they reached Cusco, with its buildings of gold and silver, they melted down the precious metals and sent them back to Spain. To strengthen their position as the new rulers of the region, the Spanish destroyed many of the Incan buildings and reused the stones to build their own cathedrals, churches, and government buildings.

Yet Machu Picchu shows no sign of destruction. Archaeologists are certain that the Spanish never reached the city and were not responsible for the abandonment of the site. One sign of this is that the Hitching Post of the Sun, the Inca's most sacred site, remains intact. The conquistadors destroyed other signs of Incan religion in Cusco and at sites across the Sacred Valley.

DOWNFALL OF THE INCA

The overthrow of the mighty Incan Empire by a small band of Spanish adventurers is one of the most extraordinary stories of world history. When Francisco Pizarro and his men, backed by Spain's rulers, arrived on the coast of Peru, they found an empire divided by civil war. Many of the people in the empire had been conquered by the Inca and did not really support them. When it seemed possible that the Inca might be overthrown, many of these peoples

LEFT: *Atahualpa greets Francisco Pizarro in this modern re-creation of their first meeting .*

turned against their rulers. But local support alone was not enough to guarantee Spanish victory. There was also a remarkable coincidence.

A HELPFUL LEGEND

An Incan legend told that one day a god would appear as a pale-skinned and white-bearded man. Pizarro's appearance matched the description exactly. Perhaps the Inca thought that he was a god in human form.

Atahualpa, the Incan king, treated Pizarro with great respect. The Spanish repaid Atahualpa by taking him hostage. They said that they would release him in return for a huge ransom of gold and silver. The Inca collected the ransom—but the conquistadors killed Atahualpa anyway. His brother, Manco Capac, fled to the hills of Vilcabamba.

Still, there were only about 200 conquistadors facing thousands of Incan warriors. But the Spanish had many advantages. First, they brought about sixty horses with them. The Inca had never seen horses before and were afraid of them. The conquistadors had guns, while the Incan weapons were swords and spears. Perhaps most deadly, however, were the diseases brought by the Spanish. Most Europeans had a resistance to the diseases—but the Inca did not. Smallpox wiped out much of the Incan population.

After the Spanish captured Cusco, the Incan state collapsed. The Inca fled to the remote hills. Manco Capac and his

ABOVE: *Descendants of the Inca celebrate the Inti Rayma festival in Cusco by wearing traditional clothing and carrying samples of the foods that supported the Incan empire, such as corn and potatoes.*

descendants resisted the Spanish until 1572. They ruled their own kingdom from Vilcabamba. In 1572, however, the last Incan ruler, Tupac Amaru, was captured and executed by the conquistadors.

Today, archaeologists are still discovering hidden Incan sites. These sites were probably part of a system of linked cities. The splendor of Machu Picchu suggests that it may have been the center of the system. It is possible the Inca abandoned the site because of a lack of water. Many Incan settlements were located on top of steep hilltops where water was scarce. In periods of drought, the Inca could well have been force to leave.

LIVING TRADITION

The descendants of the Inca, the Peruvian Indians, continue to live in Cusco. They still speak Queche, the language of their ancestors. They continue to celebrate the magnificence of the Inca. Each year on June 24, local people celebrate *Inti Rayma*, a festival dedicated to the Incan Sun god. Dressed in the traditional clothes of Incan priests, nobles, women, soldiers, and messengers, local people honor the Sun god in the streets of Cusco.

Interpreting the Records

The Inca had no written language. They kept records by using knotted strings called quipu. Today, no one can interpret quipu. Our knowledge of the Inca instead relies on accounts by the Spanish and on Incan ruins and artifacts.

One-sided records are a problem for archaeologists. It is impossible to tell if they are accurate. Some conquistadors wrote about the Incan Empire. Many painted the Inca in a bad light and praised the conquerors. Others criticized the Spanish government. *The Conquest of Peru*, completed in 1615, was addressed to King Philip III of Spain. It protested the treatment of native Andean people by the Spanish conquerors. Its author, Guaman Poma de Ayala, was a Peruvian who spoke and wrote Spanish. His account, and those of other critics of Spanish rule, became known as *leyendas negras,* or black legends.

ABOVE: *Quipu recorded everything from taxes to censuses. Today, no one knows precisely how to decode quipu.*

WHAT DOES THE FUTURE HOLD?

MACHU PICCHU ATTRACTS VISITORS FROM ALL OVER THE WORLD, BUT THE VISITORS MAY ACCIDENTALLY DAMAGE WHAT THEY COME TO SEE.

About 3,000 visitors make the trip to Machu Picchu every day. The site is one of the most popular tourist destinations in the world. But its popularity is also its biggest problem. Walking the Inca Trail to Machu Picchu has become so popular that only 500 people are allowed on the path each day. The others must travel by train.

BELOW: *So many people want to visit Machu Picchu that numbers have to be limited.*

More tourists bring more trash. Their feet wear away the ground, no matter how carefully they walk. Archaeologists working at Machu Picchu and along the Inca Trail understand that tourists are a necessary part of modern life. However, they are concerned that the needs of the visitors will get in the way of **excavations** that are still revealing the secrets of Machu Picchu.

LEARNING FROM TECHNOLOGY

When Bingham explored Machu Picchu at the start of the twentieth century, everything was done by hand, and local people worked only as laborers. Today, the archaeologists working at the site include Peruvians as well as many other nationalities. Technology has revolutionized archaeology. Computers can analyze data much faster, and photographs taken from **satellites** in orbit around the Earth help archaeologists to understand the many sites around Machu Picchu and the connections between them. Experts use handheld GPS (global positioning system) devices to record precise information. Remote sensing techniques allow experts to "see" what is under the ground without having to dig it up. Even so, physically exploring sites is still invaluable to understanding them.

Radiocarbon dating has helped experts understand more about the crops the Inca grew. The main crop was maize, or corn. It was so important that the Inca had gold and silver carvings of corn in the temple at Cusco. Corn was the staple food, and was also used to make *chichi*, the maize beer.

EDUCATING THE GRAVE ROBBERS

Another important tool for archaeologists is education. By teaching local people about their ancestors' achievements, they want to encourage them to take pride in their past—and to help preserve it. Local support might help protect Machu Picchu and other sites in the Sacred Valley. In particular, it might reduce the problem of grave robbers.

Grave robbing is particularly serious in Peru. Museums and private collectors around the world have obtained artifacts

SOS: Save Our Site

In 2000 the Peruvian government announced drastic measures to protect Machu Picchu. The following year, new rules came into effect. The number of hikers who could walk the 28-mile (45-km) Inca Trail was limited to 500 a day, and they could only travel as part of an organized tour. Plastic water bottles were banned on the trail to avoid trash. Pack animals for carrying supplies were forbidden. The fees for walking the trail and for visiting Machu Picchu were raised to discourage visitors.

The government hoped the stricter rules would reduce the impact of visitors along the trail. However, it is clear that the measures have not worked. There has been no decrease in the annual number of visitors to Machu Picchu.

BELOW: *A raise in the ticket price for Machu Picchu has failed to reduce the number of visitors, so other controls may be required.*

RIGHT: *The pathway leading up to Machu Picchu has existed for centuries, but it is being rapidly worn away by the feet of modern hikers.*

from professional robbers and smugglers. The problem is being tackled on an international level. Governments are prosecuting museums and museum curators who are involved in illegal trade in ancient artifacts. Italian authorities accused Marion True of the J. Paul Getty Museum in Los Angeles, California, of acquiring looted art. In 2007, True went on trial in Italy for conspiring to deal in stolen artifacts.

EXCITING TIMES

By involving the local community in preserving Machu Picchu and by controlling the number of tourists who visit, archaeologists hope to buy time to allow for a more complete understanding of the site. These are exciting years for archaeologists studying the Inca. Over the last couple of decades, there have been some important discoveries in Peru. In Tupac Amaru, a town north of the capital, Lima, archaeologists excavated a vast Incan cemetery amid the slum dwellings. High in the Andes, meanwhile, archaeologists who work at high altitudes have found a number of well-preserved frozen bodies left as sacrifices by the Inca. Such new discoveries, together with the continuing work at Machu Picchu and other sites, are helping archaeologists better understand the complex workings of the Incan Empire and its sudden fall.

Further Resources

BOOKS

Baquedano, Elizabeth, and Barry Clarke. *Aztec, Inca, and Maya.* New York: DK Children, 2005.

Gruber, Beth. *Ancient Inca* (National Geographic Investigates). Washington, D.C.: National Geographic, 2007.

Peterson, Sheryl. *Machu Picchu* (Ancient Wonders of the World). Mankato, MN: Creative Education, 2005.

Somervill, Barbara A. *Machu Picchu: City in the Clouds.* New York: Children's Press, 2005.

WEB SITES

Ice Mummies of the Inca
http://www.pbs.org/wgbh/nova/icemummies/

Ice Treasures of the Inca
http://www.nationalgeographic.com/mummy/

Peru Cultural site on Machu Picchu
http://www.machupicchu.perucultural.org.pe/ingles/index.htm

UNESCO World Heritage Machu Picchu site
http://whc.unesco.org/en/list/274

Virtual tours of Machu Picchu
http://www.destination360.com/peru/machu-picchu-cb.php

Glossary

align: To position a structure to line up with certain points.

archaeology: The scientific study of cultures by analyzing remains such as artifacts and monuments.

artifact: An object that has been made or changed by humans.

astronomy: The scientific study of the movement of heavenly bodies such as the stars and planets.

conquistador: Spanish for "conqueror."

elevation: The height of a geographical feature above sea level

empire: A large area of many peoples ruled by one emperor or empress.

excavation: A scientific dig to explore an archaeological site.

foundation: The part of a structure that is sunk into the ground to support the rest of the building.

heritage: Beliefs, buildings, and objects left to a people by their ancestors.

loot: To steal treasures from old tombs, usually to sell.

monument: A structure meant as a lasting celebration of a person, event, or other subject.

mummy: A body that has been deliberately or accidentally preserved.

murals: Images painted directly on walls.

puma: A wild cat that was sacred to the Inca and other American peoples.

pyramid: A structure that rises to a point from a four-sided base.

radiocarbon dating: A form of dating that analyzes how much carbon has decayed in objects that were once alive.

ritual: A ceremony carried out as part of religious worship.

sacred: Something worthy of worship.

sacrifice: An offering to the gods, sometimes involving the killing of an animal or a person.

satellites: Objects that are launched into space to orbit around the Earth.

tax: A contribution paid by a citizen to the government for the services provided.

theory: The explanation that best fits the available facts.

Names to Know

Bingham, Hiram (1875–1956). American archaeologist who brought Machu Picchu to the world's attention. Bingham later served as a U.S. senator.

Savoy, Gene (1927–2007). American writer and adventurer who discovered more than forty Incan sites in Peru.

Index

Page numbers in **bold** type refer to captions.